Lerner SPORTS ROOKIE

SOCCER MANIA

BEST MEN'S SOCCER PLAYERS

Cara Krenn

Lerner Publications ◆ Minneapolis

For Luke

Statistics in this book are accurate through August 1, 2024.

Lerner Publications Company
An imprint of Lerner Publishing Group, Inc.
241 First Avenue North
Minneapolis, MN 55401 USA

For reading levels and more information, look up this title at www.lernerbooks.com.

Main body text set in Mikado. Typeface provided by HVD fonts.

Editor: Nicole Berglund **Designer:** Viet Chu **Photo Editor:** Nicole Berglund

Library of Congress Cataloging-in-Publication Data

Names: Krenn, Cara, author.
Title: Best men's soccer players / Cara Krenn.
Description: Minneapolis, MN : Lerner Publications, 2026. | Series: Lerner sports rookie. Soccer mania | Includes bibliographical references and index. | Audience: Ages 5–8 | Audience: Grades K–1 | Summary: "Who are the greatest men's soccer players of all time? Young soccer fans explore male legends of the sport, including Diego Maradona and Lionel Messi"— Provided by publisher.
Identifiers: LCCN 2024037533 (print) | LCCN 2024037534 (ebook) | ISBN 9798765668368 (library binding) | ISBN 9798765683729 (paperback) | ISBN 9798765681053 (epub)
Subjects: LCSH: Soccer players—Biography—Juvenile literature.
Classification: LCC GV942.7.A1 K74 2025 (print) | LCC GV942.7.A1 (ebook) | DDC 796.3340922 [B]—dc23/eng/20240916

LC record available at https://lccn.loc.gov/2024037533
LC ebook record available at https://lccn.loc.gov/2024037534

Manufactured in the United States of America
1-1011707-53804-10/18/2024

Table of Contents

Soccer's All-Time Best Men

Lionel Messi races up the field.
He receives a perfect pass.
He kicks the ball toward the net.

Goal!

Soccer is the world's most popular sport. Millions of people play and watch it.

The top athletes play on pro teams. They may also play for their country's national team.

INSIDE SOCCER

Soccer is called football in most countries.

The top tournament is the World Cup. Teams from many countries compete to win. Some World Cup players stand out as the best of all time.

INSIDE SOCCER

The first men's World Cup was in 1930. It is held every four years.

Pelé won three World Cups for Brazil. He scored over 1,000 goals!

Franz Beckenbauer played strong defense. He also scored a lot of goals. He won the World Cup for Germany as a player and as a coach.

Johan Cruyff played a type of soccer called total football. He won many awards.

INSIDE SOCCER

Total football is when any player can play anywhere on the field.

Diego Maradona could run fast and dribble the ball. He played in four World Cups for Argentina.

Maradona scored the Goal of the Century. Some people think it was the best goal ever.

Diego Maradona

Cristiano Ronaldo is one of the world's most famous players. He plays forward. He has scored 132 goals for Portugal.

Lionel Messi has won eight world's best player awards. He led his team to win the 2022 World Cup for Argentina.

AFA
10

Watching the best soccer players is exciting. Who do you think will be the next all-time best men's player?

Glossary

defense: a position that stops the other team from scoring

dribble: to move the ball with the feet

forward: a position that scores the most goals

Learn More

Krenn, Cara. *Best Women's Soccer Players*. Minneapolis: Lerner Publications, 2026.

Ludlow, Roberta. *Lionel Messi: A Little Golden Book Biography*. New York: Golden Books, 2024.

Wagner, Zelda. *Soccer Superstars*. Minneapolis: Lerner Publications, 2025.

Index

Photo Acknowledgments

Image credits: AP Photo/Marta Lavandier, p. 5; AP Photo/Frank Hoermann/SVEN SIMON/picture-alliance/dpa, p. 7; AP Photo/Jonathan Huff/CSM, p. 9; Focus On Sport/Getty Images, p. 11; AP Photo/Werek/picture-alliance/dpa, p. 13; PA Images/Alamy, p. 15; Aflo Co. Ltd./Alamy, p. 17; AP Photo/Andrzej Iwanczuk/NurPhoto, p. 19; AP Photo/Bagu Blanco/PRESSINPHOTO/Sipa USA, p. 21; MesquitaFMS/Getty Images, p. 23 Design elements: vid64/Getty Images; boytaro Thongbun/500px/Getty Images.

Cover: Florencia Tan Jun/PxImages/Alamy.